HOW TO ENSURE
SUCCESS
in Project Leadership

The 5 Practical Leadership Habits
to Become a Highly Valued
Project Manager

David Romero, PMP

How to Ensure Success in Project Leadership
Copyright © 2017 by **David Romero**

All rights reserved

ISBN-13: 978-1974158836
ISBN-10: 1974158837

Dedication

This book is dedicated to Rocío, Diana y Jorge. Together we have worked on the most passionate project possible, learning of the secret of a purpose-filled life.

Your present, full of energy, revitalizes me.

Your future, full of opportunities, motivates me.

Because you deserve that I give you the best of myself, I seek to become the best version of myself that I can be, both personally and professionally.

To my parents, without whose raising this book would not have been possible. The people who taught me the value of patience, perseverance, and action. First things first, and then the rest.

To my sister, united by love and blood, and by your constant support.

Contents

INTRODUCTION

Never before in history have there been so many professional possibilities. Practically any professional goal can be achieved these days. New advances in technology are what make this possible.

Nonetheless, it must be made clear that I do not wish to say that new technology will serve our professional objectives to us on a platter, not requiring that we do anything or next to nothing to achieve them. In this way, new technology facilitates goals and opportunities, but when it comes to reaching our objectives the main ingredients are the same as always; these are focused work, perseverance, acceptance of failure, order, clarity, integrity, and more.

This book's objective is twofold; on one hand, it is so you can obtain the best results on a project and on the other so that you reach your maximum professional potential. This is a book specifically centered on project leadership since it is the only way of achieving both objectives. Providing people with leadership is the key to success and between these people you are also there.

Leadership is not being a boss; it is being able to get the best out of every individual. It is setting an example. Leadership is not simply directing, but rather serving and inspiring those around you. Being a leader means being the flame that lights the fire that beats inside every human being. It is being the breath that helps others to continue forward. It is being able to open the minds of everybody, teaching them and helping them to go on a fascinating journey. It is not working harder or working more. It is getting the best out of everyone. Work done by people working together, and who have the desire to reach their full potential, creates the best results for a project. When a group of people join together on the path towards maximum potential, the best project results possible is what occurs.

Leadership depends on you and how you influence others at work and help them to develop. Your attitude is evaluated by your peers and it is they who decide whether you should be a leader.

Leadership requires attitude, purpose, growth, inspiration, action, humility, obligation, confidence, courage, reflection, integrity, authenticity, and discipline.

We cannot improve by doing the same thing again and again; that's why it is important to open your mind to new approaches.

"It is not easy to stop thinking- as we have always done-, however, it is impossible to improve –by thinking as we have always done-".

THE FIVE HABITS

"Only through leading yourself can you start to lead others, not the other way around"

Welcome to a new perspective on project management that has the potential to completely change your results. I would appreciate it if you let me share the five habits that have been key to my professional development with you. When you apply them, I am sure you will obtain the best project results.
I hope they end up being as important for you as they have been and are for me.

Let me start with a question. Have you ever felt like the image? Have you felt that you are trying a lot but achieving very little? I felt that way for years.

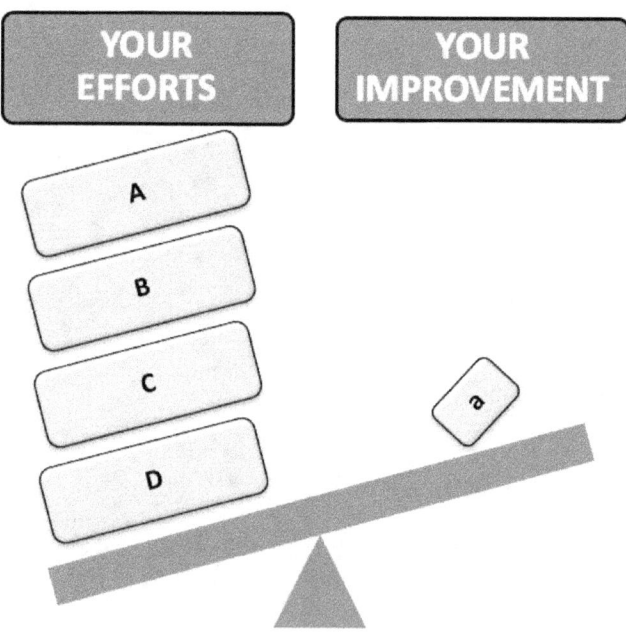

For years, despite considerable efforts to improve, my progression was slower than I wanted. I struggled a lot, but my improvement was minimal. That is, the relationship between my effort to improve and my actual improvement was very unbalanced. I took courses, read books and watched online classes,.…..

In the life of every professional working on projects, a moment comes when we feel we can scarcely improve.

At this moment, you feel you are missing something, although you know that you have it deep inside you. Has this happened to you? Possibly, it has. Now I will explain how to go beyond this moment for better success in your projects.

The majority of professionals make the same mistake, one so important that it determines their professional limit and as a result, their projects' level of success.

During my first years as a professional, I thought that the better I was technically, the better my technical skills were, the nearer I would be to achieving my maximum potential and achieving better results. Like many other professionals, I believed that technical skills were everything. My focus was 100% based on technical skills.

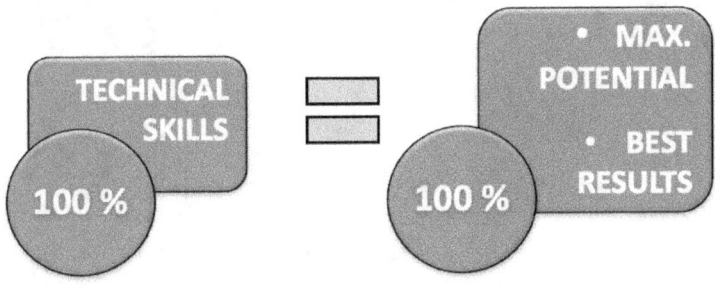

It took me years of effort and mistakes to understand that my attention to leadership skills had been zero. 0% as you can see in the picture. I was only considering half of the equation. I realized that if I continued to concentrate exclusively on my technical skills, although I had developed them to 100%, I could not achieve more than 50% of my maximum potential.

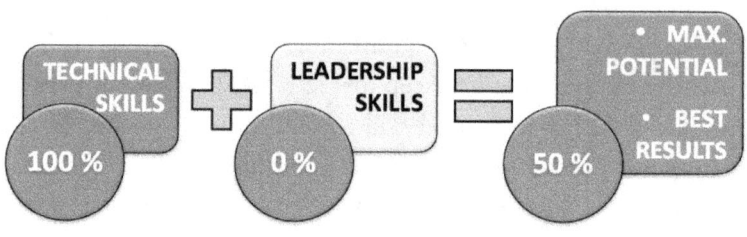

When I realised the importance of leadership skills, my aim became the following equation:

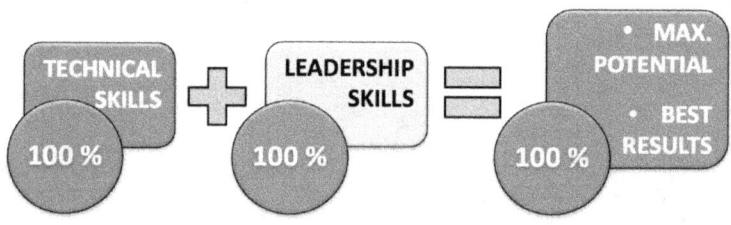

The equation is that you can only reach your maximum potential and thus the best results in the project if you fully develop your leadership skills as much as your technical skills. Since we usually focus disproportionately on technical skills, I will always say that "The success of a project is based on one´s leadership."

In this visual example, I am giving equal value to technical skills and leadership skills so that it is easier to explain and understand.

Regardless of the value that you think that leadership skills have versus technical skills, it is vital to understand the great importance of leadership skills in your results. It is evident that project success comes from development of our technical skills and from the development of our leadership skills also. Both should be developed. Experience tells us that we should mainly develop our leadership skills; those are what we tend to leave aside in favor of technical abilities.

Let me add more evidence. A few years ago, the PMI published a report under the title Navigating Complexity from a macro survey directed at professional project management worldwide. The question was, what are the most important skills to successfully manage highly complex projects?

The result was overwhelming. For 81% of the successful organizations (high performers), leadership skills were the most important when it comes to successfully managing complex projects. 81%. In contrast, only 9% considered technical skills as the most relevant, 9% strategic and business skills and 1% other.

The reported concluded by saying that professionals with highly developed leadership skills can manage projects and programs with high levels of complexity.

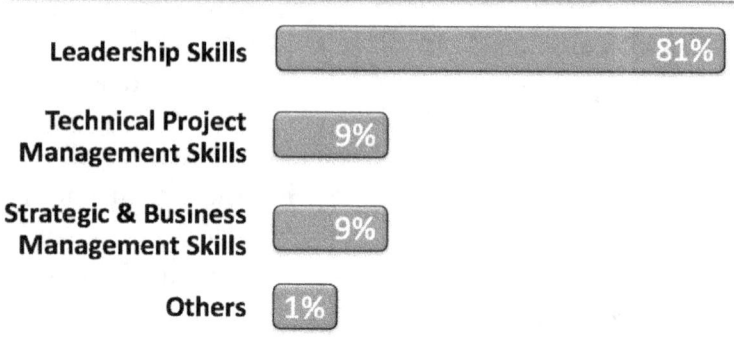

Most Important Skills to Successfully Manage Highly Complex Projects

Skill	Percentage
Leadership Skills	81%
Technical Project Management Skills	9%
Strategic & Business Management Skills	9%
Others	1%

If that were not enough, not long after that survey, the PMI revised its Continuing Certification Requirements program. They placed leadership skills as one of the three sides of the Talent Triangle, and thus skills that require training to maintain certifications.

Now, I want to ask you: Are you going to start considering leadership skills as your next area for improvement? I hope so.

At this point, you are already aware of the importance of leadership skills. Now you may ask, **what are these leadership skills?**

Although there are a multitude of leadership skills, ... to be humble, trustworthy, disciplined, ... you need not be an expert in all. You may wonder, which of these skills should I develop specifically?

To lead a project, you must develop an **adequate** and **indefinite** number of leadership skills. I repeat, adequate and indefinite, because your team members will recognize you as a leader based on your actions. No company can grant you the gift of being a leader. I want you to get rid of the idea that to be a leader is to be a boss, or a manager, or a director or a person in charge. This does not make you a leader…. you can only be the leader when your team - based on your actions - recognizes you as the LEADER.

> *"The team appoints the leader as a result of your attitude and your leadership style, not your company"*

FOUR AIMS, FIVE HABITS

To achieve your best results in your next project, I will present the 5 fundamental habits that will help you to improve your leadership skills.

Since the success of the project is the result of team effort, each one of the **5 habits focuses mainly on an agent of the project**.

The focus of the **first habit** will be on the most important part of the project: **the TEAM**. The success of the project depends on the team, and getting to know the story of each person is vital.

We will move onto the **second habit** and place our focus on **the CLIENT**. The project exists because there is a client; and is developing a very specific relationship so that we can exceed the client's expectations.

In the **third habit**, we will find the best results and new opportunities for **the COMPANY** and will enable team **growth** in an unusual way.

The **fourth** and **fifth habits** are focused on **YOU personally**. Therefore, in the fourth habit we talk about a particular attitude that lets you achieve new and better achievements. We end with the fifth habit, where we learn what we must do to guarantee constant growth, thereby ensuring robust professional and personal development.

Thus, TEAM, CLIENT, COMPANY and YOU are the four aims on which the five habits focus, that will allow you to improve your leadership skills and be successful in the project.

4 AIMS	5 "ABSTRACT" HABITS
1. TEAM	"STORY"
2. CLIENT	"RELATIONSHIP"
3. COMPANY & TEAM	"GROWTH"
4. YOU	"ATTITUDE" "DEVELOPMENT"

Let's begin with the first habit.

HABIT #1: GET TO KNOW EACH PERSON'S STORY

"A leader doesn't focus on an individual's performance but on an individual's potential"

I always say that "We tend to believe that 'being busy' doing whatever, is more important than 'knowing the people' who could make a difference in the project."

What do you know about the people in your team? and How important do you think it is to get to know the members of your team?

In this first habit, you will learn:

- Why it is so important to learn the story behind each person and

- How to get to know it

People who have others under their responsibility often make the mistake of putting them to work before they have developed a relationship of value with them. We feel the need to avoid wasting time and immediately start working.

However, a leader knows that **before getting to work,** they should establish a **special connection** with the members of the team. A leader is responsible for building a strong relationship that provides security and encouragement to each member of the team, because that is the way to get the best results.

What I call 'the story of each person' is that personal story full of success, failures, and personal goals to achieve.

Experience tells us that it is easy to connect with a person on a high level after learning their personal story. We connect naturally through our own personal stories. That is the keystone.

BENEFITS

We are beginning to know why it is so important to learn each person's story.

First of all, it **improves the working environment.** When you show interest in each person's story, you convey 'You matter to me,' and as a result the people feel more in tune. When we are in a good working environment we feel like we matter, that our work matters, and the outcome of the project depends on us. People feel a sense of gratitude and we return it by doing a better job. A good working environment is essential to achieve best results for the project.

Second, **individual skills** are **used more effectively**. When you show interest in the stories of each team member, you realise that each person is different. Each person has his or her own experiences and expertise. Only when you understand the uniqueness that each person can bring, you can make the most of each person's skills and strengths during the project.

Third, when you figure out the **expectations** and **motivations** of each person, what they would like to do, how they would like to do it, this is when you can align people and projects.

In summary, when you learn the story of each person, you convey to the team members `you matter to me´, you align their motivations and expertise with the projects and the results improve substantially.

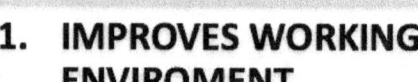

IMMEDIATE BENEFITS:

1. **IMPROVES WORKING ENVIROMENT**

2. **INDIVIDUAL SKILLS ARE USE MORE EFFECTIVELY**

3. **ALIGN PEOPLE AND PROJECTS**

HOW DO WE LEARN THE STORY?

To learn more about each person, we should have face-to-face meetings with each of them. This is how we can get to know and understand each person, find out what they like, and what interests them most about their professional career. This is how we enable stronger and trustworthy relationships.

So let's see, how do we learn the story of each person?

I learned and experienced this lesson by chance. I was working for many years as a project manager and my work began to prove to be relatively easy. It gave me more time to reflect on team development, which is how I discovered what I now call 'the great questions'. These are the questions that allow one to learn 'the story behind each person'. I divide these "great questions" into two big groups so that they are easier to remember.

The aim of the first group of questions is to **get to know the professional each person has become from all his or her experience.** It is important to make clear that I do not look to know about their CV, what they have worked as or how many projects they have participated in. This is more a level of 'the lessons and personal experiences that have shaped the professional' that person has become: Let us see some examples:

- What made you choose this career path?

- What is one of the lessons that you usually tend to remember?

- In which project have you learned the most? And why?

- What project do you feel most proud of and why?

- Tell me about a team experience that you found rewarding.

- Have you ever had difficulty working with a manager?

- In what parts do you think you have been the most useful for the team? For the project?

- What has motivated you the most?

- What was special about the project team that provided you with the best results?

- What was the best professional with whom you have worked like?

I repeat, the aim of this first group of questions: is to get to know the 'the lessons and personal experiences that have shaped the professional' that person has become. The responses give us information about strengths, weaknesses, personal opinions, areas of possible improvement, areas where people would especially like to work, motivations, and more.

On the other hand, the aim of the second group is to get to know their **future professional motivations.** Some examples are:

- What about your career path motivates you the most?

- How would you like to stand out and be recognized as a professional?

- How do you think that you could add value to the result of the project?

- What are your professional goals for the next few years?

- What is something you have never done that you would like to do one day?

- In what field would you like to improve?

- If you could learn one new ability, what would it be?

- How do you think you add value to projects?

- How could you make a difference on this project? How can I help you?

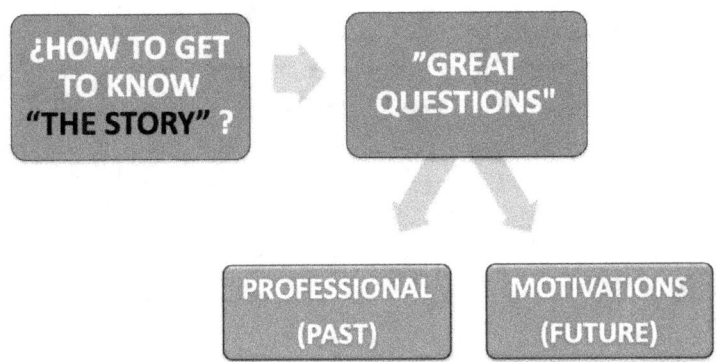

These types of questions tend to be appealing, because we are not easily accustomed to asking them or responding to them. This is only at the beginning. If you insist, you and the other person will become accustomed and will achieve answers that will surprise you.

In my personal experience, the formulation of those questions not only helped me when leading the project, but, surprisingly, was also a benefit for all of the team members. For example, questions helped to the team members:

- To understand better their importance and their role within the team and the company.

- Questions also served as motivation to achieve better results.

- And, something very important, much like the image that these people have of themselves, the company's image of these people radically changed for the better. Why do they benefit from this? Because the questions help us to better understand and therefore make better decisions.

SUMMARY

Here is a summary of the habit 'getting to know each person's story.'

Most people tend to believe that to begin carrying out tasks as soon as possible is more important than getting to know the people who could make a difference in the project. It is because we aim not to waste time.

The truth is that when we start the project, learning about each team member's story:

1. We create personal connections that create a better working environment.

2. We can align the motivation, strengths and expertise of each person in the project.

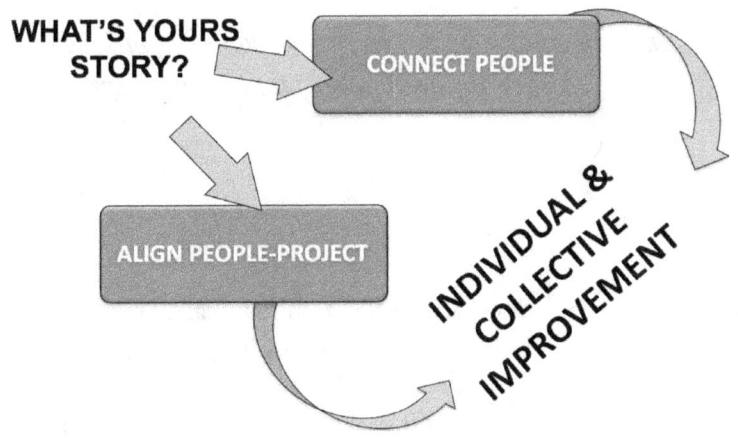

We should look to maintain personal relationships that create what I call the 'great questions.' When we create these questions, it makes one think 'you value me.' A person who feels that he or she matters has much more motivation and can put that into the team. Without a doubt, in this sense, the project will start in a better way. We should keep up face-to-face meetings where we formulate what I call 'great questions.' When we formulate these questions, we make them feel 'you matter to me.' Everyone who feels that 'they matter' feels a big motivation and they will put it into use for the team. In this way, without a doubt, the project will start better.

When you begin to put this habit into practice, you will start to understand that:

> *"The true quality of a leader is not found in his or her knowledge, but in the development that he or she produces in others"*

To produce this development, we must learn 'each person's story.' So why not start tomorrow by asking, for example:

- What project do you feel most proud of and why? and see how discussion develops.

HABIT #2: A VISION BEYOND THE REQUIREMENTS

"Without a vision, you will navigate towards an uncertain goal and you will get no more than an average result"

It is very simple, "Without a vision, there will be no success in the project".

Naturally, we focus on the project's requirements and, based on them, we immediately start to work on the project. On rare occasions, we work to create a vision beyond the requirements. This is one of the biggest mistakes we can make. In this chapter, we will leave behind, our confused idea about the vision, going beyond the requirements of the project. I guarantee you that the vision of the project will be different than what you believed.

LET'S SEE

You have probably carried out many projects that have fulfilled all of their requirements, right? However, on how many of these occasions did you feel that from the client's perspective, the project wasn't successful? More than once, right?

Let me make it clear that if the client does not consider the result of the project a success, the project is not a success. You have only met the contractual requirements.

It is important to create a vision, because without it we cannot go beyond the requirements. This naturally translates, from the perspective of the client, into the failure of a project.

Fulfilling 100% of the requirements ...
DOESN`T
guarantee the success of the project

" The project is a success
when...

... the client succeed"

We usually believe that we know what we have to do, but without the vision, as we will see, it would be impossible to have a successful project. The vision of the project is much more than knowing the requirements.

After a few years, I realized that when we just focus on executing the required tasks, the project never ends in a success because the result does not provide the client with added value. You may wonder, why should you provide added value?

I have, too often, seen "what the client thought that he needed" did not match what "the client really needed," despite meeting the project requirements, it resulted in a bitter victory. For this reason, we need to find what the client really needs, their actual needs, and add that value.

Only when we manage and lead the project **considering the success of the client,** can the project be a success.

In order to have a successful project, we should not work so that we obtain formal acceptance on the deliverables from the client. Focusing on fulfilling the triple constraint of time-cost-quality does not guarantee success.

Remember that the project will succeed only when the client deems it successful and that occurs only when we meet **the real needs of the client**. That is to say, the success of the project does not provide what the clients think they need, but what the client really needs.

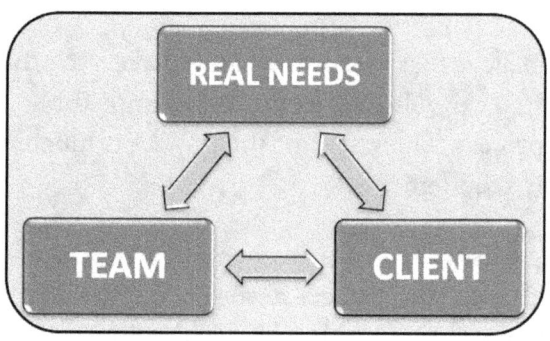

The success of the project depends on...
finding the real needs of the client"

In this respect, the former director of marketing for Apple, Guy Kawasaki says, "People cannot describe what they need from a company. All that they can say to you is that they want something bigger, quicker, and cheaper than what they already have". It therefore seems obvious that we must help the client to find what they really need and create it. This is the only way we can succeed in the project.

The key to this habit is to be able to align the team with the client and the real needs of the client and thus to be able to exceed client expectations. Why exceed their expectations? Because there is something the client does not know they need.

Partnership team-client

¿How? ...

... "Exceeding expectations"

HOW TO EXCEED EXPECTATIONS

Now let's consider the process of being able to exceed client expectations.

The first step is very easy. It consists of not starting to execute tasks until after we have created a shared vision with the client. It's that simple.

The second step consists of changing our mental status quo of being on an inferior level, in which we strictly carry out the assigned tasks, to one in which we play more of 'partnership' role to the client. For this I speak about the creation of a 'team-client' association, because from our expert position we will find what is best for the client.

The third step is the most exciting and where we do most of the work. The client's company has a vision. The client has a number of needs to be addressed in order to achieve that vision. Thus, the project emerges, in a client requirement.

We are also going to create a vision, although in our case it will be in the project. Our aim is to learn as well as possible the vision of the client's business. That way, we can adapt the project to the client's real needs.

Our project, in blue, is one of a series of projects, white circles, which the client needs to implement to achieve their vision.

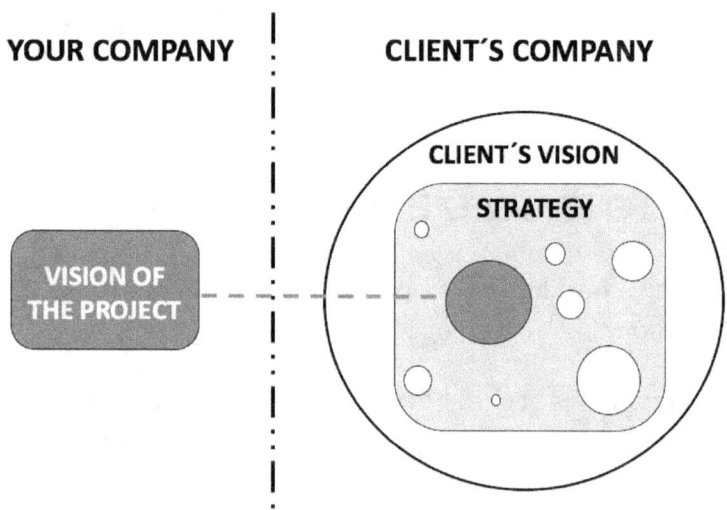

All of those projects, which are certainly aligned, are part of the 'client strategy'. Therefore, in order to achieve success in the project, we must not only focus on what the client has requested us to do, but we should understand the client's business. And this includes knowing as well as possible the client's vision and strategy. Only then, can we discover the real needs of the client's business.

Obviously, to understand the business and the client's needs we should hold various meetings and ask lots of questions. For example, do you know how your project is aligned with the goals of the client? It will be necessary to collect relevant information.

To help you remember the type of questions, I have divided them in three big groups.

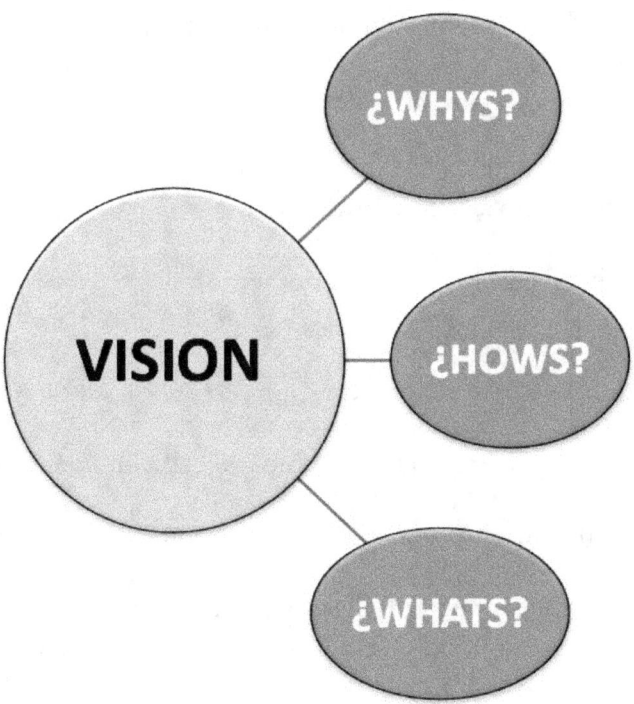

The first group is based on the **"Whys?"**:

- Why does the client want us to do the assignment they have given us?

- Why is this project interesting for the client? or Why now and not later?

The second group is based on the **"Hows?"**:

- How will the result of the project be integrated into their business?

- How will this project benefit your company?

- How would you briefly summarize the reason for this project's existence?

The third group are the **"Whats?"**:

- What other steps contribute to their strategy to reach their vision?

- What could we do to improve the project?

- What are we going to do to align the project with their vision?

- What are the business goals the project is aiming to achieve?

- What business benefits will these goals deliver if achieved?

By knowing the background of the project from the client's perspective, we can achieve two fundamental things:

1) We will be able to run a project that meets the **real needs** of the client.

2) We will find it easier to **exceed the client's expectations**.

Align project with .....
Client´s business

- ## Real needs

- ## Exceed expectations

¡¡ Project success!!

Now surely you understand the importance of building a project vision beyond the requirements based on the client's business. Of course, you will understand me completely when I say, "without a vision there will be no success in the project".

SUMMARY

By developing and implementing a project with good time, cost and quality, we will probably have complied with our contractual obligations. Is this enough for the client to be satisfied? Probably not.

The important thing isn't to finish tasks. Since the client often does not know everything that they need, if we focus exclusively on what we think that the client wants, we won't be successful in the project.

To do this, we must know in depth the business of the client, providing what they do not know that they need, exceeding expectations.

It will be necessary to spend time with the client to gather important information that allows us to align the project with the client's business and help them to materialize their vision for their company.

Now, do you still understand the vision as you understood it before?

Tomorrow, ask your client:

What other projects are you working on? And what do you expect to achieve in those?

HABIT #3: ENABLING THE GROWTH OF THE TEAM IN AN UNUSUAL WAY

"The essence of a leader is not searching for personal success; a leader ensures the success of the rest"

This habit is based on facilitating the team's growth so that the company grows.

Success can only be achieved through a group effort, not through individual effort; that's why an authentic leader searches for the success of the whole team and not their own individual success. In this respect, I would like to ask you:

If we don't enable the growth of the team, how can we face bigger challenges and get better results?

In this third habit, you will learn how the growth of the team is enabled. I'm sure it will surprise you.

Let's start. When we talk about the enabling the growth of the team, we usually think about......empowering and more specifically... delegating tasks.

Unless you are able to do all of the work of the whole team by yourself which you will not be able to, you will have to delegate tasks, which is nothing more than... assigning tasks. However, DELEGATING does not guarantee results, so is delegating enough? The answer is no.

When a manager delegates, it is a one-way communication. Delegating is authorizing someone to do a job,.... But it does not involve the key, which is TRUST.

When you **trust**, the team understands that their work matters and that they matter. When a manager trust, two-way communication is produced, trust in both directions is made possible and that is the first big difference.

So the team is not limited to doing their job carrying out tasks, rather they look for the way of producing better results, because they feel indebted. And why do they feel indebted? Because trust helps and allows the team to grow professionally.

Therefore, the key is not to **delegate** because this alone does not produce better results. The key is to communicate **trust**.

Despite the obvious differences between delegating and trusting, a difference exists above all of them. Let me explain to you.

When we delegate, we don't communicate trust because we are **afraid of making mistakes**.

We usually only delegate by assigning simple tasks, but we do not communicate trust. The reason is because we are afraid of making mistakes, so the team does not grow and it stagnates.

However, and this is the big difference, when we trust, we **accept mistakes** as part of the process of the project. When you trust, you allow the team to make their own decisions because you **accept mistakes** as a transit point of the project. Trust allows you to assign more complex tasks and even tasks that are out of the depth of individual team members, and as a result the team feels important, the members work to their best abilities and grow, and thus the results exceed the expectations.

Moreover, trust results in powerful motivational influences. Let me explain to you:

1) When someone trust in ourselves, we feel **responsibility**, and this motivates us.

2) When someone trust in ourselves, we realize the possibilities of what can be **achieved**, which is motivation.

3) When there is trust, we see the possibility of being **promoted**, and that also is motivation.

Trust provides independence to the team and so the team grows. The company benefits because it is ready to confront major challenges.

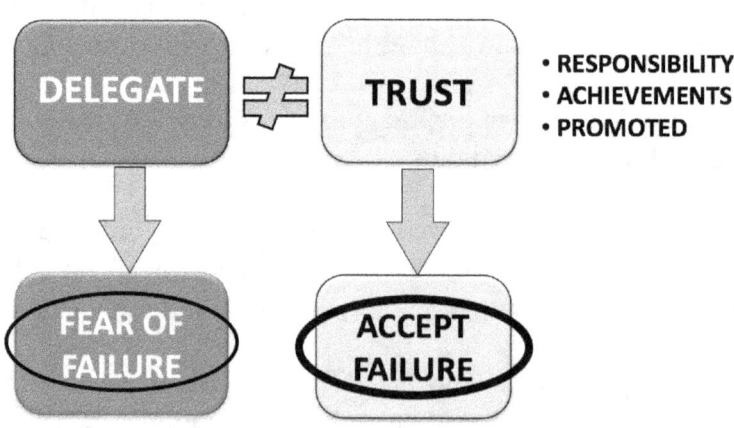

I agree that it is difficult to accept mistakes. However, since the differentiating factor is accepting failure, I think that it is necessary to help eliminate the **fear of making a mistake** right now.

Mistakes must be assimilated as just another phase of the project, although it may be a phase that we don't know when it is going to happen. In other words, mistakes are not the end of the project. Mistakes are the stage whereby the majority of the biggest results need to happen.

Some time ago, I discovered that there are two ways to make a mistake in the project:

1) One is when you make a mistake and it is all over. It is over because you have decided that is it over, not because it is written or someone is telling you. This is the only way a mistake becomes failure.

2) The other way of making a mistake is considering the mistake as a value. This is because it helps you to take a new direction, refocus yourself and go more precisely and directly towards your objectives.

We would all like to never make a mistake. But what happens if we make a mistake before the achievement? Will it now no longer be achieved? What is the objective, to avoid making a mistake or to achieve the objective? When we are closer than we have ever been to achieving what we want, why leave it?

Since you are going to make mistakes, in what way would you like to make the mistakes? Make mistakes and give up, or make mistakes moving ahead?

Remember that:

> *"Mistakes are not failure unless you decide that they are"*

The mistake is part of the process, so don't be scared of making a mistake.

> "Being defeated is often a temporary condition. Giving up is what makes it permanent"
>
> - Marilyn vos Savant

TIPS

From now on, I hope that you stop **delegating** and start **trusting**. However, you may be concerned that if you trust it means giving a blank check to everything. The answer is NO. It is not to say, "do as you please." I recommend 3 things:

1) Firstly, the context must be drawn, explaining how the task is set within a bigger image. You must be clear and specific about the results that are wanted.

2) Secondly, you must check that it is understood. The simplest and most effective thing is to ask the team about

the results they hope for and afterward open a round of questions.

3) Thirdly, you need to understand that all action must correspond with the vision of the project and the ethics and objectives of the company.

A PERSONAL STORY

I'm going to tell you a brief personal story about how I learned the great importance of trust.

> *"Undoubtedly, when you communicate trust, the autonomy of each member improves and greater goals are more possible"*

During my second project as project manager, I indirectly learned the importance of trusting in the team, and to stop fearing making mistakes.

That project was undoubtedly the most demanding one in which I have worked.

I was overwhelmed by the amount of tasks. I was forced to focus so much on my tasks in that way, I went from micro-managing the team to necessarily trusting the team. When I trusted, the team gained the freedom that they needed. The whole team realized the opportunity to prove themselves and reach new achievements, they felt responsible for their own work and saw an opportunity to grow.

The team could use their own skills and make their own decisions, at the same time accepting it as their own responsibility.

Not only were we able to finish the project, which I personally doubted, but we also achieved a great result.

And I learned, although accidentally, the value of **trusting** against simply **delegating**.

SUMMARY

When we talk about the importance of delegating, I always say the same thing. **Delegating** is not enough, you have to **trust**. Trusting involves understanding **mistakes** as something inevitable and this leads to the emergence of powerful motivating factors.

The best results are produced in a motivating and protective environment.

Remember, "mistakes do not mean failure, unless you decide that they do; mistakes are the necessary steps toward most of the best results". When it is understood like this, trust is communicated and the results are the growth of the team, better results, and the possibility to confront greater challenges for everyone, including the business.

From now on, I would like you to start to appreciate the positive aspects of what could be your next mistake.

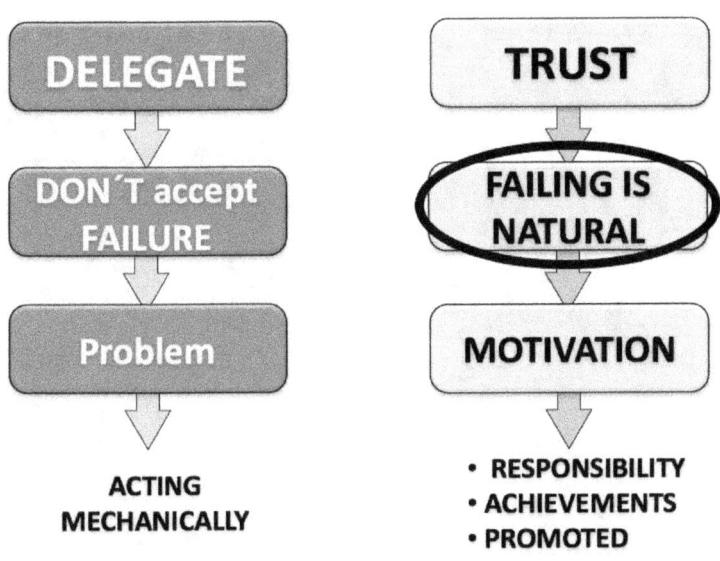

HABIT #4: THE MOST IMPORTANT OF ALL, BEING INTENTIONAL, THE KEY TO EVERY LEADER

"Sometimes the greatest gift you can give yourself is to go ahead when the easy thing would be to give up"

Intent is the attitude with which we make conscious decisions and they subsequently become reality. "The success of the project is not determined by chance, but through an intentional attitude".

Do you think that you make your decisions consciously? In other words, do you know the ratio between our conscious and unconscious thinking? If not, I assure you it will surprise you.

A study carried out by neuroscientists found that our subconscious mind makes 95% of our daily decisions. And only 5% are made by our conscious mind. It is surprising to see that we are not as logical as we thought we were. Our autopilot works for most of the day.

Thus, we can say that our subconscious mind governs us, which means that we do not tend to be very intentional. To be more precise, only in 5% of our decisions.

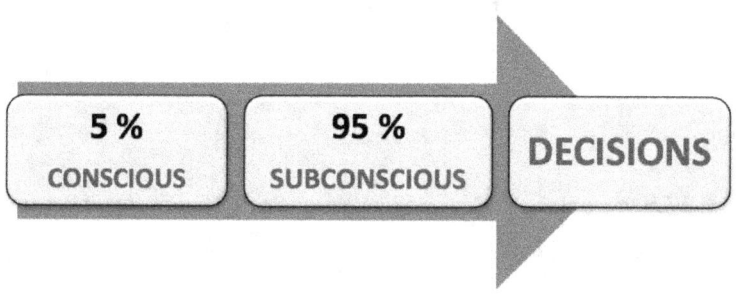

We can easily deduce from this that our subconscious mind largely determines who we are, what we do and what we achieve. It determines our achievements.

To obtain better results, it is evident that we should be more intentional. Don't you think that we should work on our subconscious mind, since it makes 95% of our decisions?

Now you will learn the key to being more intentional and obtaining better results.

BENEFITS

Let's start by listing some of the benefits. Being and acting intentionally allows us:

1) To be able to achieve all of the objectives that we have set ourselves.

2) To continually grow and set ourselves greater challenges.

3) It also acts as a powerful contagious attitude for the team.

BEING INTENTIONAL

We live in a time of great efficiency, in which processes and mechanization are our daily lives. We perform most of our tasks automatically; in other words, we do not have any intentional behavior. We are busy even though, frankly, being busy does not involve intent. We simply limit ourselves to completing tasks, often working like robots and therefore barely being intentional.

When we do something without intention, nothing changes and we obtain the same results over and over again. The truth is that being intentional does not consist of working more, but of working more intelligently.

A simple way to understand "intention" is that:

"Intention is the bridge or attitude that links where you are with what you want to achieve."

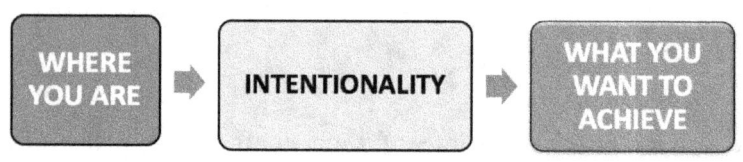

It is the attitude that allows you to achieve anything. When we are intentional, we achieve any goal.

An intentional project leader starts from the final image of the product or service as a map of the path toward the end goal, instead of simply carrying out the tasks that are expected to be done.

KEY INGREDIENTS

What key elements define being intentional? There are two:

The first key element, differentiated from acting mechanically, and from our subconscious mind is... **Reflection**.

Intent requires reflection. **Reflection** allows us to move ourselves away from living mechanically. It moves you away from the life in which you question nothing and continue doing things that you think are expected of you and in a way they have always been done.

Intent is applicable to all aspects of our projects; it is an attitude. "Being intentional is not doing things for the sake of it; it is a conscious act" because it involves having initially reflected. Reflection is an enemy of automatic work because it considers other alternatives.

When we become intentional, we search for and find out how to reach our goals.

Secondly, being intentional requires **Action**.

We need Action to turn what we previously thought into reality, our conscious decisions. Intent and action are inseparable.

Action is often the differentiator because it involves moving away from the classic "modus operandi" of doing "things that have always been done in the way that they have been done", from the "we'll see what we will do"…

EXAMPLES

Some simple examples of intent? Putting into practice some of the habits that we have seen requires intent.

- When we keep up meetings with members of the team, to know the story of each person, we are being intentional.

- When we are looking for the real needs of the client, as we have seen in the 2ⁿᵈ habit, we are being intentional.

- A different example of the habits seen is, for example, when planning a meeting in advance to convey a message, we reflect on the following:

  ➢ What do I want them to know?

  ➢ to feel? And

  ➢ to do?

You are being intentional because you have first reflected on what you are looking for and because second, you will have put it into action.

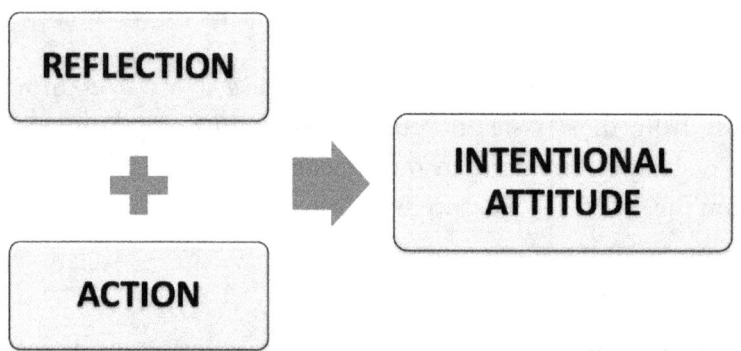

SUMMARY

Being intentional is the habit that I particularly consider the most important and a differentiator. It is not just a habit, but a key ATTITUDE in a leader. Intent allows us to achieve our goals.

Based on scientific research, we learned that our subconscious mind makes 95% of our decisions. We are governed by autopilot and this way we obtain the same results over and over again.

The keys to intent are two things:

The first is reflection…What do we want to achieve? Why do we want to achieve it? What are we going to do? Afterwards the second key, action, is in charge of transforming our reflection into reality.

My advice is for you to be intentional instead of being carried away by the flow of day to day life. Stop acting mechanically and try to think "outside the box" to be able to achieve any objective.

You must be intentional in all areas of the project to have success, with the team, with the client, with partners, stakeholders, companies…

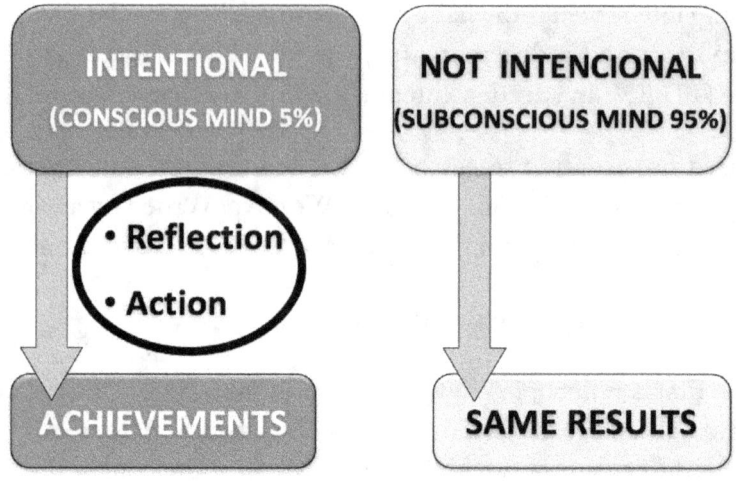

Being intentional takes time. However, when you assimilate it, it will be your natural way of working and so you will be able to achieve anything. Furthermore, you will become an example and an example is highly contagious, your team will benefit from it, and you will obtain better results.

I suggest that today you ask yourself, what objective do you want to achieve tomorrow? Set the objective today and do it tomorrow. Ask yourself the same question every day.

> *"Leadership begins with oneself and purpose is one's guide"*

So these are the 4 habits that will provide you with project success. Further below, you can read a summary that compiles everything we have seen. But, is applying these four habits enough?

Undoubtedly, if you put these 4 habits into practice, the results of the project will improve exponentially and will guide you towards your maximum potential.

What is true is that I would like you to reach your full potential as quickly as possible. Your maximum potential does not require other people, rather it is achieved by focusing exclusively on you. For that reason, in Habit #5, I present you with three simple disciplines that will allow you to develop your potential.

HABIT #5: DEVELOPING YOUR FULL POTENTIAL

"Don't take personal growth for granted but as daily and conscious development"

THREE SIMPLE DISCIPLINES

Years ago, I realized that putting the four habits into practice made achieving the best project results possible. At the same time, however, the development of my full potential was slow. I understood that developing our potential required other ingredients. I realized that "leading is not a destination, but a daily routine".

When I say that leadership is a daily routine, I say it because it requires constant growth on our part. It must be continuous growth because there is no final destination, and because we live in a world that is constantly changing and at a great speed. Developing our potential requires continuous growth.

This continuous improvement rests on the daily application of a series of disciplines. But what disciplines should be chosen, when there are hundreds? Most disciplines seek to obtain more efficiency at the workplace, better relationships, better results… and the majority of them can help us to a greater or lesser degree. Nonetheless, the main problem is that we have little time to try them, digest them, and introduce them into our habits.

Like you, I too worry about losing time; that is why I always look to achieve more with less. I believe the secret is not to practice many disciplines that allow us to grow, but rather to employ the lowest number of them that produce the best results with the least amount of effort. That is why I present to you three simple discipline that will help you in developing your full potential.

These are the three simple disciplines that have had the greatest impact on my persona and my results:

The **first** discipline is **READING**

As Margaret Fuller said, "Today a reader, tomorrow a leader".

If I had to choose only one thing out of all those that help you improve professionally and personally it would be, without a doubt, reading. We must feed our minds to move forward, and I have found that the best way to do that is to read.

Basically it is good for three main reasons:

The first one is that reading helps us to think better. The truth is that reading improves and promotes reflection. When you read, your mind collects valuable information that goes on to form part of your thoughts, message, and communication.

The second reason is that reading helps us to speak and therefore express ourselves better because reading increases our vocabulary and teaches us new things. Therefore, reading enriches our conversation.

The third one is that reading provides us with new perspectives that stimulate our growth with regards to new ideas.

Other aspects that are benefitted are our mental health when we enjoy reading.

In my opinion, almost every type of reading is good, even if it is not related to your professional field; this is because it provides you with something that others do not. Above all, I would advise that you not focus solely on technical material related to your profession.

The **second** discipline is **REFLECTION**

In my opinion, "Reflection expands our comfort zone and leads us to the place where one finds our true potential".

Reflection is a fundamental discipline because it allows us to escape from working like an automaton. We disconnect from the daily routine and therefore it allows us to grow and reach our full potential. Regarding this, Dan Rockwell of Leadershipfreak always says that, "You don't grow when you are working; you grow when you rest and reflect".

What to reflect upon? It is interesting to reflect on what you do and what you do not, about what has happened to you and what has not. You can reflect on your work, social life, family, or your life in general.

When it comes to reflection, one of my favorite questions to ask myself is what have I learned today? And, how can it benefit me? These questions help me to gain a better understanding of things and make the most of my day.

Reflecting only ten minutes per day allows you to take control of important decisions. The practice of reflection begins with a strange feeling for the first few days, but after that it becomes one of the favorite parts of the day.

The **third** discipline is **PHYSICAL EXERCISE**

Maybe you are wondering how can exercise help me grow? It has been shown that as little as 20 minutes of physical exercise:

1) Stimulates brain plasticity and facilitates the increase of new neuronal connections.

2) Reduces stress levels and acts as an anti-depressant.

3) Releases endorphins, producing a sense of well-being.

4) And, improves our general physical as well as mental health.

5) Furthermore, in my personal experience it has meant the best moment for inspiration, the moment when I have come up with my best ideas. I have realized that when you go running for a bit, the effort needed results in me losing control over my mind due to having to dedicate a large portion of physical resources to the exercise itself. In this manner, my mind is freed and provides me with new ideas.

Without a doubt, most of my best ideas have come while exercising. In case you are not the exercising type, taking a twenty-minute stroll will serve you just as well. There are no excuses and many benefits.

SUMMARY

To summarize, we already know that leading is not a destination, but rather a daily labor; this is because we need to continuously improve and develop ourselves. For that reason, we have taken a look at what in my experience are the three most important disciplines when it comes to improving oneself.

There are many others, nonetheless these three will help you to create a good foundation upon which to rest your growth. The three disciplines that I advise you to follow are:

Reading: This is the discipline that will help you the most to grow.

Reflecting: Just ten minutes a day will improve reasoning.

Exercising: This will help you keep your mind and body in shape.

> "A time comes when you need to stop waiting for the man you want to become and start being the man you want to be"
>
> - Bruce Springsteen

SUMMARY OF THE FIVE HABITS

"You have to be able to influence yourself before you are able to influence others: that's essentially the leadership process"

Now it is time to summarize what we have seen up until now.

We started with the formula that will allow us to achieve better results in the project. It is important to improve our technical abilities, but we can only achieve better project results when we develop our leadership abilities.

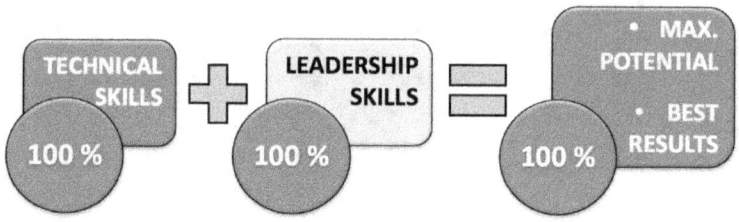

Later, we were introduced to the report of the PMI survey, in which 81% considered leadership abilities as the most important in succeeding in the project. We also saw that leadership abilities have ended up becoming one of the three sides of the PMI triangle of talent.

Having understood the relevance of leadership abilities in order to succeed, we learned the 5 key habits to achieve the best results.

4 AIMS	5 "ABSTRACT" HABITS
1. TEAM	"STORY"
2. CLIENT	"EXCEED EXPECTATIONS"
3. COMPANY & TEAM	"TRUST & GROWTH"
4. YOU	"INTENTIONALITY" "DEVELOPMENT"

> *"A big part of the success of our transformation comes from our determination to acquire new habits"*

In the **first habit**, we concentrated on the team and we saw the importance of knowing the STORY behind each person. This is the first step we should take. It is the best way to build an environment that produces better results for the project. Knowing "each person's story" contributes towards the connection because it conveys the message "I care about you" and allows you to align people and project.

In the **second habit**, we concentrated on the client. If the project is not successful for the client, it will not be successful for us either. We saw that, when we concentrate on the business of the client, we are able to align our project with their business. The client does not usually know everything that they need to, so if we concentrate solely on what they want, we won't be successful. Therefore, we must find the real needs of the client, and thus be able to exceed expectations.

In the **third habit**, we promoted the growth of the team for their benefit and the benefit of the company, and we did it by giving the necessary **trust**.

Delegating tasks does not involve trust, so good results are not guaranteed. Instead, you should build trust in the team, because trust produces motivating factors for the team such as responsibility, achievements, and the possibility of promotion.

The key to building trust happens through accepting mistakes as part of the process of the project. This way, the team will be able to grow, the company will be able to confront bigger challenges, and everyone will achieve better results.

In the **fourth habit** we concentrated on the essential characteristic that every leader must develop in **intent**.

I particularly consider it the most important quality of a leader, since it enables you to achieving any goal. It stems from **reflection** and finishes with the main ingredient, which is **action**, which continually makes goals reality.

Is putting the four habits into practice enough? Undoubtedly, the use of the 4 habits will allow you to achieve better results in the project. And that's a lot!

Nevertheless, having reached this point we are not satisfied with obtaining the best project results. We also want to develop the best professional version of ourselves. That is why **habit #5** focuses on **our personal and professional growth** in order to achieve our full potential. Remember that I always say that, "Leading is not a destination but daily routine". This is because it also means continuous personal growth and development.

For this reason, I have proposed the three growth disciplines that, without any doubt, have personally worked for me the best:

- Reading

- Reflection

- Physical exercise

REFLECTIONS ON THE FIVE HABITS WHICH WE HAVE FAMILIARIZED OURSELVES WITH

"A leader doesn't have all the answers but has the courage to make the best decision"

STORY

- When you know the story of every member, you know the human being that exists between the professional world and the private one.

- You cannot speak of vision if you have not connected with each team member beforehand.

- You cannot speak of vision if you have not met every team member beforehand.

- You cannot speak of vision if you do not know what inspires every team member beforehand.

VISION

- Without vision there is no journey towards the project's success.

- Vision means reflection, which is the fundamental element when it comes to connecting, trusting, being intentional, and growing.

- When you create the correct vision, you establish your team's, project's, and client's destination.

TRUST

- Every professional hopes that others will trust them to show their worth.

- When you trust, you fill each person with the most powerful fuel known to man, confidence.

- Confidence inspires us and provides us with the impetus needed for great results.

- Confidence is what allows us to continue on at the worst of times and be successful at the best of times.

INTENT

- A project cannot be successful without intent.

- When we work with purpose, our team embarks on a journey to a place where the best results are produced, where our limiting thoughts are overcome.

- When you work with purpose, you establish yourself as a great role model for others to follow.

DEVELOPMENT

- When you grow, you push your limits and establish new destinations.

- Experience itself does not guarantee growth. We grow when we are aware of the necessity to grow, in the areas that benefit us the most, and at the time that benefits us the most.

- We do not grow simply because time goes by; we grow when we have gained the necessary clarity and have implemented that clarity into our daily behavior.

- Growth is the healthiest, most rewarding, and most successful mental practice that a professional can initiate.

LASTLY

"To lead takes more than desire. People need to see value in you and nothing speaks louder than your actions"

Before finishing, I would like to make you aware of something that will happen to you and what you should do when it does. You already have a good understanding of how to have a positive impact, using the four objectives that we have focused on, on the TEAM, CLIENT, COMPANY, and YOU.

The truth is that at some point during the process, you will stumble; do not expect to be perfect the first time around. When it occurs, because it is not a question of if but when, remember that stumbling is not the end. True, it hurts but it is also true that it is the step that most great results must experience. It often happens when we face the unknown, right on the path towards the project's success. It is also found on the path to development and growth.

Furthermore, I want you to understand that all significant and important progress requires **Perseverance**.

I always like to explain it with the following quote from Steve Jobs: "I am convinced that half of what separates the successful entrepreneurs from the unsuccessful ones is pure perseverance".

As you could imagine, the path towards your better results, in which you should develop your leadership abilities, will involve high doses of perseverance. If you make sure that you grow (despite the fact that at times you will be stumbling) and you persevere, you will be successful.

Act. The more you expose yourself and put into practice what you have learned the faster you will grow. Action is the only way to achieve anything. "Do not expect to know everything, just begin with the first step".

"Change will not come if we wait for some other person or if we wait for some other time. We are the ones we've been waiting for. We are the change that we seek"

-Barack Obama

Any achievement begins with the decision to take the first step towards the unknown. Do not put off improvement. Think today what you will do tomorrow from the moment you get up. Out of everything that has been read, what can you begin to put into practice tomorrow?

We have arrived at the end of this book. I hope that you decide to improve your leadership abilities. My wish is to leave you with two clear main ideas:

I. The first is that "the success of the project is based on one's leadership". Do not doubt it.

II. The second is that "leadership is the result of a personal attitude that inspires others to succeed".

Thanks

My acknowledgment and gratitude goes to you, the project professional who tirelessly seeks to be the best they can.

I like meeting people of a similar nature to myself, people who make mutual understanding simple.

It makes me happy to know that you recognize what leadership really means. Using your effort and that of your other colleagues, we can share our passion for achieving seemingly impossible goals and contribute to the growth of others.

The reason for this book is you. My mission has been to share my experience with those who share my concern and motivation, which is to achieve our full potential in our field, project management.

It is possible in the future we will be able to work together. Never rule out that possibility. Whether or not that happens, I hope that you maintain that desire to stand out from yourself, always.

My best wishes,
David Romero

The author

David is a project management and leadership consultant, trainer and coach and the founder of Intentional Project Leadership.

As a project management professional, he's been certified as PMP and has been recognized as a global authority on project management leadership.

He specializes in helping professionals to assimilate leadership skills, so they can take a step up in their career while their company attain its better project results.

He is a fully qualified personal development coach and a founding member of The John Maxwell Team in Spanish.

He is an active PMI volunteer and is a cofounding member of Aragon Branch of PMI Madrid Spain Chapter and Toastmasters Zaragoza.

He is also the author of "Alcanza tu Máximo Potencial en la Gestión de Proyectos".

Intentional
Project
Leadership

UNLEASHING THE LEADERSHIP SKILLS YOU HAVE AND NEED TO SUCCEED
David **Romero**

www.ingramcontent.com/pod-product-compliance
Lightning Source LLC
Chambersburg PA
CBHW071228220526
45468CB00002B/768